The Biggest Motorbike Joke Book Ever!

Over 300 Funny Motorcycle Gags for Bikers of All Ages

Danny Trevanion

Copyright © 2023 by Danny Trevanion

All rights reserved.

No portion of this book may be reproduced in any form without written permission from the publisher or author, except as permitted by U.K. copyright law.

This work is not authorised, endorsed or associated in any way with Dorna, FIM, MotoGP, MotoE, World Superbike, British Superbike, Motocross or any of their companies and franchises. This book is simply a joke book about the subject of motorbike racing.

Contents

Introduction	1
Motorbike Jokes	8
MotoGP Jokes	93
MotoE Jokes	121
World Superbike Jokes	126
British Superbike Jokes	131
Motocross Jokes	136
The Finish Line	141

Introduction

This book first started because of my love of MotoGP. I started writing jokes well over a year ago, and then one thing lead to another, and I before I knew it I was writing general motorbike jokes too. It turned out I had enough material I could look at working my way to another joke book.

I have loosely followed MotoGP most of my adult life up until 4 years ago. In

2019 I seriously got into MotoGP. I was mesmerised by each round and the drama on and off track. That year was the last time Marc Marquez won the championship title. This was not unexpected at the time as he is one of the greatest aliens ever to ride a motorbike. However, his tragic injury in Jerez in July 2020 really upset the predictably of the race. During covid and lockdowns, the crowds trackside might not have been great but with spectators like myself at home, my attention was more availably than ever before. In conjunction with the racing closer than ever, and the variety of different race winners, the eventual champion Joan Mir only won a race at near the end of the season.

The next year my level of interest grew even further and I started watching Moto 2 and Moto 3 more avidly each race weekend. To be surprise and delight, many of these extra races were more entertaining than the feature race. Moto 3 especially has a special madness that makes for an engaging spectacle. Fabio Quartararo won a solid victory in 2021.

In 2022 I was so hooked I started watching free practice sessions on the

Friday, which I had previously found rather dull. I could finally start seeing the nuances, learning about the technical information, set up of the bikes and tyres. Later on in the season, it became a two horse race with Quartararo failing to perform at his previous top level, leading to Francesco Bagnaia taking the 2022 title.

This year I got so into MotoGP I started writing jokes. That's when I know I'm really interested in a subject, which you will know if you've read any of my other niche joke books. The introduction of sprint races has me watching more racing than ever before, and even with this I have found it has only increased my love of racing. My hunger for motorbike racing has gone so far to get into World Superbikes and British Superbikes much more than any other year. Although I am not as knowledgeable about those as MotoGP, I am watching each weekend with the same great enthusiasm.

I make it no secret now, as although I enjoy many other sports, some of which I will release collections of jokes about in the near future, including Formula One. MotoGP is not only my favourite motorsport, but my number one sport.

I've recently been playing the official video game, which is the hardest PC game I've ever played, and the realism is superb. And I've played a fair few, even writing the biggest book of original jokes on the subject. I'm persevering with it, but the learning curve is steeper than the Waterfall at Sachsenring.

In this collection you will find many motorbike jokes for different classes and general ones. As with all my books, some jokes require a deep level of knowledge about the subject. If you don't understand it, you can use your favourite search engine, or email me: dannytrevanionjokes@gmail.com or find me on social media @dannytrevanion. I can't promise to explain how my mind works but I can try and give it a go. Equally, if you don't find a joke to work for you, move on to the next one, and the next one after that. Hopefully, you'll find some to your liking that you can share with others.

I hope this book will give you a few laughs between the thrills of the racing.

Danny Trevanion

November 2023

Motorbike Jokes

A rider walks into a bar.

"What will it be?" asks the barman

"Some human fuel, good sir"

"We don't serve that. On yer bike!"

Why did the bike mechanic change the wheels?

Because of the way they spoke to him

What do you call a Harley rider that's a complete pig?

A road hog

What do you call a Harley that spins it's wheels but does not go anywhere?

A Groundhog

What do you call a Harley that spins it's wheels but does not go anywhere on infinite loop?

Groundhog day

What do you call an angry bike race?

Motocross

What do you call a pacifier riding a motorbike?

A crash test dummy

Did you hear about the motorbike rider who got drunk in the paddock?

He was completely leathered!

Why did the racer run out of space on track?

Because there was too much *vroom*!

Why was the motorbike rider born in a stable?

Because there was no *vroom* at the inn

Why are the best riders like the tail-end of

their bikes?

Because they exhaust all options.

What music do riders avoid when they crash?

Heavy metal

Why was the rider always going to his trailer?

He was mastering the art of breaking

Why did the baker put new tyres on his bike?

To make the more impressive doughnuts

What do you call a old rider that's been riding in the rain?

Rusty

How does a rider wash their clothes?

On a spin-cycle

What did the lion say when it got run over by a motorbike?

Nothing. It just let out a little roar.

Why are angry rider dangerous?

They fly off their handle bars

How do riders engage with social media?

    They put a handle on it

How do you ride a mini-moto?

    Handle with kid gloves

How does a rider eat?

    Only with their forks

How does a rider like to fly?

    In a chopper

What do you call a sad rider doing doughnuts?

Moped around

What do you call a motorbike in the morning?

A dew-cati

Why are Americans riders surprised when they eat sweet potatoes?

Because they're Yam-aha!

What bike do a monkey ride?

A Hairy Davidson

What do you call a laughing motorbike?

Haharly Davidson

What bikes do dairy farmers ride?

Cowasaki

Which bikes are safe for drink driving?

Kawasaké

How do you alert pedestrians when riding in Japan?

With your Honkda

What bike does Burger King ride?

A Royal Enfield with Cheese

I rode a Norton when I was sick and now I'm virus free.

Why is a steady rhythm important to slowing down?

Because of hitting the drum brake

Why do riders hate slowing down?

It brakes their heart

What type of riders love the sound of their engine's purring?

Du-cat-i

What do you a bike-lover obsessed with their journey?

A motorcyclepath

What's the different between a BMW bike and a BMW car?

About 30 grand

Which manufacturer makes the ultimate winning machine?

Victory

Why do riders wash before they race?

So they can get a clean start

What do you call a rider lingering on the

racing line?

An accident waiting to happen

What do you call a motorbike taking a nap?

A snooze-suki

Why is a motorcycle museum like a amusement park?

Because you want to ride them all

Which motorbike sounds as sweet as honey?

A BeeMW

Which motorbike is mediocre?

An OKTM

How do fast riders communicate?

Zoom!

What do riders call it when their having relationship difficulties?
 They've hit a gravel patch

Where do Italian riders carry their olives to be destoned?
 Pittted lane

Where do mechanics make their clever remarks?
 Witlane

Where the riders rest should be nicknamed sitlane

How does a rider eat their yoghurt?

With great Muller Corner entry...and tipping the topping in first.

Why is rhythm key to winning?

Because a ridet cab beat the other to the line

What do you call an orange part of a track?

Pithlane

Free practice seems oxymoron for how a rider pays for not getting into Q2

Where do riders go to consul themselves?

Pitylane

How does a rider play water music?

Using his Handel bars

How is getting up to speed like a boxer's flurry of punches?

Because they both go through the gears

What do you call riders who also love walking?

Motorhikers

How do you say goodbye to a rider?

    Motorbye!

What do you call riders who can read your mind?

    Motopsychs

How do riders show their approval on social

media?

　Motolikes

What fish do rider catch?

　Motopikes

Why are subscriptions to lightweight bike so cheap?

　Because riders get a free-trial bike

What do you call a riding championship with only one track?

MonoGP

Why did the bike fall over laughing?

Because of it's kickstandup comedy

Why is a bike engineer's job so hard?

It's not sprocket science

What is the cleverest part of a bike?

Bright spark plugs

What is the lazy way to extend a bike?

With brake padding

What do you call a bike that's just exited from the pits?

Running at fuel capacity

How does a rider protect themselves from farts?

With a windscreen

Why did the rider race without his helmet?

   So he could get a head start

What do you call a loose pannier?

   A chatterbox

What do you call it if you break apart a bike's cylinders?

A chip off the engine block

How do Hell Angels show their loyalty?

With their bad side mirrors

What is the mental structure of a rider?

A motorbike frame of mind

What are Batman and Robin called when they ride the Batbike?

The Aerodynamic Duo

What did the rider keep gazing in his side mirror?

He had something to reflect on

What's the great thing about getting new filters?

    You get a clean brake

What do you call clean tail after a race?

    An exhaust pipe dream

What   goes

"bump...whoosh!...bump!...whoosh!....bump!"

A rough with a smooth ride

What do you call a fatigued rider with a puncture?

Flat out tyred

How does a tyre get wealthy?

With inflation

What motorbike do kids ride?

A goatacycle

Why did the bike wheel get in trouble?

It spoke out of turn

How does a rider slow down on corner

entry?

   Curb their enthusiasm

How does a rider keep on track?

   On their noteabike

Why did the rider forget to do a clean lap?

   .Because the track had lost it's marbles

Why does a rider eat halloumi before qualifying?

To do a squeaky clean lap

When does a rider realise their ego has inflated too much?

When the airbag goes off

Why do riders make their law to listen to their bike's body?

To give it a fairing hearing

What do you call sponsorship on the bike's body?

A fairing-ing endorsement

What does you ride when you want to take the scenic route?

A detouring motorcycle

What is the best advice for a duck after a crash?

Get back in the waddle

How does a rider know when their bike seat is worn?

It gets saddle

What do you call a bike from Top Gun?

A Tom Cruiser

How does a rider keep to schedule?

With their rotabike

How does a rider take a selfie?

On their photobike

What do you call a rider who throws shapes on corner entry?

A brake dancer

What happens a bikes geometry is misaligned?

The rider will get out of shape

What does the fastest rider do on a clean lap?

Leave the others for dust

What did the motorbike say to the car?

    Are you four wheel?

What do you need most to be a championship rider?

    Great motorvation

What do you call a rider with one eye?

Motorcyclops

What does George Foreman ride?

A lean mean motorcycling machine

Where does a rider get their knowledge?

A Motorcylopedia

How does a biker stop riding?

    Break the cycle

How does a rider stop riding?

    I told you..."brake" the cycle

I haven't ridden in such a long time but I'm told it's just like riding a bike

What does a biker need after a hot lap?

A ride on a motorcycool

What does a biker ride in windy weather?

A motorcyclone

Who can't shut up about their new bike?

A motor mouth

What does a politician ride?

A mayorbike

Why does turning off an electric bike lower the mood?

Because if's a buzz kill

What does a castle ride?

A moatorbike

Why was the sailor motorhead confused?

He didn't know they should travel on their boat--or-bike?

What does a rider leave when he drops his kids off at a swimmimg pool?

A floaterbike

Who gave birth to the first rider?

The motherbike

What do ghosts ride?

A polterbike

What do you ride if you want to male no noise?"

Muterbike

I know a rider who wanted to know his better so suchb dov he had a handlebar mustache on his bike's handlebars.

What do bikers use to be heard?

A motormike

What does Shaggy say when seeing Ghostrider?

MotorZikes Scoob!

What does a rider shout when they're about

to crash?

    Motoryikes!

What does the Grim Reaper ride?

    A Motorsickle

What herb do all riders need to get to get better?

    Track thyme

What do riders need when improving on lap times?

1Gain tracktion

What do the stewards give when the track is invaded by ducks?

A quack limits warning

Which way do the riders follow?

    Race direction

What's the important skill in a rider's strategy?

    Making tracktical decisions

What do riders have for breakfast?

Wheelybix

How do extreme riders fill their tanks?

Fuel throttle

They say I'm a silly and immature biker but that's just ride-diculous.

My hog has a lot of horsepower but that's because I keep feeding it horses.

What did the rider do after a mistake?
    Start backtracking

What do riders believe when they visualise winning a race?

The law of attracktion

What do bikes ride when their in the groove?

A sound-track

What plant do riders love the most?

Root 66

My wife Hope fell off the back of my bike.

    I rode on Hopelessly

I'm arguing my bike loan.

    It's overdu-cati

Why did the motorbike cross the road?

    To get to the other sidecar

Why did the absent-minded rider take a different course to the others?

They got completely side-tracked

What's a rider's favourite game show?

Wheelie of Fortune

What do you call a biker abroad?

A motortourist

Doctor doctor, my motorbike has a fever.

Don't worry, it's only your cooling system. You just have to chill.

How does a biker cat lick the competition?

By overlapping

What do you call a biker who's riding a car circuit?

On the wrong track

What do you call a rider who gets promoted early?

On the fast track

Why did the rider go to jail?

So he could get the "inside" track

Why did the racer ride with a javelin?

To "throw" off track the other riders

Why did Ghostrider break suddenly?

So he could stop other riders dead in their

tracks

When do riders feel the burn of the other riders?

When they're hot on their tail

What do you call an rider on an American track?

A COTAbiker

What's the best to bike jump on for laughs?

A jokeabike

What do you call a bike that stops water?

A motordyke

Why do bikers eat quickly?

Because of motorbiting

What is a rider's favourite shoes?

    MotorNike

What disease can effect a racer's results?

    MotorBlight

How does a rider go to the toilet?

They go MotoPP

What does a new mechanic when they notice rubber degradation?

Tyre where?

Why did the rider pour porride over the track?

To race his oaterbike

Where does a Geordie racer lose time?

    Tyre and Wear

How can you tell if a rider has been sick?

    They're wearing racing green.

How does a rider win in the wet?

    They s-lick the competition

What can be said about a rider who does stunts through the night?

They burnout the tyres at both ends

Where do bikers party?

At the motorcycle club

What's more adorable than a scooter?

    A scuter

How does a rider eat?

    Using telescopic forks

What part of the bike do Bill and Ted like mosy?

Schwing arm

What do you need to attach to a bike when it rains?
　A swimarm

What is the name of the gratitude campaign?
　Thank bike!

Testla have started making electtic motorbikes. Apparently it's unique feature will be it's Elongnomic geometry.

What do you call a pirate who has theur leg stuck n their bike?

Footpeg leg

What game do biker's play to save their bacon?
Road Rasher

Did you hear about the new movie about motorbike turning? It was a wheel flop.

What do you call a biker eating fruits and

nuts during recess?

    Trail mix breaking

With a motorcycle license you can also drive a three wheel car - if you wheely, wheely, wheely want to.

What do you call a biker who fights for their rights of their tyre?

    Taking a wheelstand

What does a biker get when spending too long in an enclosed motorcycle?

Cabin fever

What does a biker want who wants bigger fairings?

To make their motorcycle more streamlined

What does a biker use to slow down the tempo of their music?

    Compact disc brakes

Why is a chatty biker like a driveshaft?

    They're all torque

How do you cheer up a motorbike?

With a motorcycle lift

186. Where do bike transport live?

The motorcycle trailer park

What do you call a bike stuck in the mud?

Anything you like, it won't help to move it.

After selling his bike, he wouldn't stop complaining about how he missed the feeling of the wind in his hair. So, for his birthday, his wife bought him a fan for his birthday. He was annoyed and wouldn't stop complaining about that either. So at Christmas his wife bought him a wig, which shut him up.

How does a biker make fast payments?

With a supercharger

Did you hear about the biker who only ate minestrone?

He rode a souperbike

What doesn't chatter but whispers?

A Pissssston

Why did the hipster biker call his bike

"Wonderland"?

He was experiencing Mad Chatter

What do bikers eat to make their safety checks regular?

Carbon fiber

Why do Australians bounce when they fall off their bikes?

Because they wear kangaroo leathers

I know if a biker who talked so much THEY experienced chatter. They didn't wear an airbag but a windbag.

Did you hear about the silly biker who avoided wearing crash helmut as they didn't want to crash?

What did the sleepy biker say to their friend in the motorhome?

Can I crash here?

Did you hear about the narcoleptic biker?

He was known as a crasher.

Why is a helmut like a poker hand?

It's safer when it's flip face down

What special treatment did Aaron Slight have on his helmut?

Anti-Foggy

Why raise a tyre when you can rear wheels?!

How did the motorbike get in trouble at school?

They were in the wrong class

What happened when the motorbike's wheels when they got old?

It re-tired

Did you hear about the mechanic who read Zen and the Art of Motorcycle Maintenance?

Their rider transcends it through their rivals

Did you hear about the giants falling from the sky onto the racetrack?

It's only men tall rain

MotoGP Jokes

Dorna are introducing a motorcycle class for cows. It's called MOOtoGP.

Rossi - the 'doctor' was so good they had to rename 500cc to MotoGP.

What do you call a MotoGP rider that wants to make a big impression?

Making a Marquez

What is it called when Marc leaves rubber on the track?

A skid-Marquez

What is a rider who plays with puppets called?

Vale of the dolls

What do you call a rider who moves other people's bikes

Vale Parking

Why does Marquez sing when he rides?

   93 problems but a hitch ain't one

What are Rossi robots known as?

   Uncanny vale

How does a Spanish rider start his race?

   On your Marquez, get set, go!

What is the rider's selfie competition?

PhotoGP

What is the best sayings competition for riders?

MottoGP

What do you call a cocktail making race?

    Mojito GP

What do you call a laughing motorbike?

    Yamahahaha

Why are motorbikes doing God's work?

    Because they have lots of revs

Why is does a rider need to consider which way to go when a part falls off the bike in front of him?

Because there's a fork in the road

How are a bike's liveries relative to each other?

They're chas-sisters

Doctor doctor! I can't stop watching motorbike racing.

I'll refer you to MotoGP

Knock knock

Who's there

Suzuki

Suzuki who?

I guess, you MotoGP guys have already forgotton us.

How many middle aged MotoGP fans does it take to change a lightbulb? Just one, but he'll spend the next hour telling you about how much better the old lightbulbs were.

How many MotoGP teams does it take to change a lightbulb? Three - one to change the bulb, one to analyze the data, and one to give feedback to the engineering team.

How many Ducati riders does it take to change a lightbulb?

Two - one to change the bulb and then his teammate to show him how to do it faster.

Imagine my surprise when I found out MotoGP wasn't racing for doctors.

What do you call the class that ride so much on the limit they scare themselves?

Moto G Pee

What degree do you get when you fail a motorbike degree?

Moto 2-2

What do you call Moto 2 called in the CEV?

    Moto 2 too

What do you call racing with magical spells?

    MojoGP

Knock knock

    Who's there?

Moto

Moto who

No, not Moto2. MotoGP.

Why are the panels on bikes attractive to riders?

Because they're pretty fairings!

The trials of riding whilst using your phone didn't last long before Dorna rejected the idea of MotorolaGP.

What are unofficial bike world championships affectionally known as?

 Not-oGP

Dorna are thinking about motorbike races on grass. It's going to be called MowtoGP.

When MotoGP stars go on tour they all request the most lavish riders.

Did you hear the next circuit is going to be on the yellow brick road?

It's called TotoGP

Cats racing motorbikes barely left the

starting grid when they tried MogoGP.

Winners of the best motorbike sound get a MoboGP award.

I thought the lean angle meant the camera had shot the rider so he looks like he has lost weight.

I got my ride height device stuck which shortened my race...all the way around.

Did you hear about the new mechanic which got in trouble? When he was told to attached aero to the bike, he stuck his chocolate bar to it.

Did you hear about the MotoGP rider who got banned from the golf club?

He tried using a hole shot device

How do you fire a biker from a team?

Get rid-er of them

What do you call the area where riders can

keep their boats?

   The pad-dock

Why did the rider join the queue of 3?

   To get inline-four

What do you call Rossi spinning his wheels?

   A spin doctor

How do you make a MotoGP bike blush?

Get marked up by a factory Ducati

Why was the rider always farting?

He was told that he needed to perfect "braking in the wind"

Why is a rider's visor like a the parent of a

boy racer?

Because they're both stuck with tearaways

What do you call an Italian motorbike that's been taken?

Apriliam Neeson

I was told the team known as KTM is actually just called "K", the TM stands for "trademark". They said K is for "kidding", but I don't know what to believe.

What do you call a team that's farted twice?

Gasgas

What do you call the parent company of a Japanese team?

Hondad

Why is the Austrian track like a energy drink pull tabs?

Because Red Bull Gives You Riiings

Where do Portuguese cats race?

Portimeow

Picture this: Dani Pedrosa racing in a virtual

reality simulator and carrying a lean angle of 46 degrees – or VR46 for short.

Why did Max Verstappen not enjoy the VR motorbike simulator?

Because it was two wheel for him

What's black, white and red all over?

A zebra on a factory Zoocati

It should be named ProtoGP as it's the premier prototype class.

What do you call Marquez's bike?

A Wonda

Why is Marquez like a gambler?

They both hope they'll be on a winning

machine

What do you call in a motorbike technician working in secret at the back of a garage?

An engine-near

What does a mechanic feel when they drop their tyre gauge?

Under pressure

What do you call the tyres on a 96 bike?

Tread Mark Marquez

What did Marquez say when he got his Ducati contract?

Marc my words, I'm ready to race!

What do you call a champion rider who

turns their season around?

They're performing Joan Mir-acles on a Honda

MotoE Jokes

Why did Ducati invest in electric bikes?

Because they wanted to "spark" some new competition!

Did you hear about the team with the shoe-string budget using dead batteries?

They tried using them because they were

free of charge

Did you hear about the mechanic who assaulted a Moto E bike?

He got charged with battery

Why are mechanics disgusted when they receive a battery that keeps shorting out?

They find them re-volting

Imagine the mechanics surprise when they unpacked the bike for the race meeting and saw read that "Batteries not included

How did the MotoE rider complain about his team?

It's all their volt!

What do you call a MotoE collision caused by bad riding?

Shocking behaviour

Why is the start a MotoE race like a national power network?

They are both electric grids

What do you call a bad MotoE mechanic?

Buzz

Why did the MotoE rider slow down ?

He didn't have enough juice

How is celebrating on a MotoE bike bad for the environment?

Because they'll be burning rubber

World Superbike Jokes

How does a rider win Superpole?

  On a voteabike

2024 sees Sam and Alex avoiding the title of the Lowest of the Lowe.

What do you call a superbiker who's crashed out of the lead?

Topracked with pain

What do you call a superbike rider who should have got a penalty?

Topracked with guilt

How does a superbiker like their coffee?

    Served by a Bautista Barista

What do you call a happy superbike winner?

    A Rea of sunshine

Who was the most graceful superbiker?

Troy Baylissom

What do you call a superbike champion who mixes up their riding styles?

Neil Hodge-podgeson

How do the best jump on a superbike?

James's Toesland perfectly on the footpegs

What superbike rider is best watched from the couch?

Tom Psyches

British Superbike Jokes

What do you call a BSB rider with low tread?

Shakey Burns Rubber

What do you call a nonsensical championship?

B.S. B

How does a policeman stop a BSB rider?

"Bridewell well well what do we have here then?"

Why don't BSB fans like Slough?

They prefer Redding

Who rides like ewe?

Leon Haslamb

What race strategies gives BSB stars advantages?

Slipstreams and slipBrookes

How does a wonky champion ride?

A little Steve Hislop-sided

What jokes do BSB fans love the most?

The Reynold ones are the best

Who is the funniest BSB rider?

Tommy Hillarious

Why does a ex-BSB rider become a commentator?

Because they're full of Whit...and Ham

Motocross Jokes

What do you call an angry bike race?

Motocross

What music does a motocross rider hear when they crash?

Rock and roll

How did the dirt rider embarrass themselves?

They soiled themselves

Why are motocross riders superior to street racers?

They're doing the dirty work

What if dirt riders collide?

That's when it really gets muddy

Why shouldn't a motocross racer park their motorhome near the fans?

So they're not airing their dirty laundry in public

Why do superbikes hate motocross riders?

Because they treating them like they're on dirt

When is it obvious a motocross rider is in the lead?

When it's clear as mud

How is Harley on a dirt track?

Happy as a Hog in mud

When is a motocross bike shamed?

When they're dragged through the mud

When is a motocross bike unhappy?

When they're kicking up mud and start mud flinging

The Finish Line

Thank you for reading this collection of motorbike jokes and puns. I truly hope you had some fun along the way and have the chance to share some of the best ones with fellow enthusiasts.

If you can consider giving this book a review, it really helps me a lot – I can't win the ranking race on my own! So if you can turbo charge my chances with a positive rating, we have a better chance to slipstream up the charts. I truly appreciate it. Thank you.

Keep laughing,

Danny

Printed in Great Britain
by Amazon